BLACK-FOOTED
FERRETS

BY JODY JENSEN SHAFFER

Published by The Child's World®
1980 Lookout Drive • Mankato, MN 56003-1705
800-599-READ • www.childsworld.com

Acknowledgments
The Child's World®: Mary Berendes, Publishing Director
Red Line Editorial: Editorial direction and production
The Design Lab: Design
Amnet: Production

Design Element: Shutterstock Images
Photographs ©: J. Michael Lockhart/U.S. Fish and Wildlife
Service, cover, 1, 4, 6–7, 9, 15, 22; Carol M. Highsmith/
Library of Congress, 5; Kimberly Tamkun/U.S. Fish and
Wildlife Service, 10, 16; Hemera Technologies/Thinkstock,
11; Shutterstock Images, 12–13; Jason Patrick Ross/
Shutterstock Images, 17; Marla Trollan/US Fish and Wildlife
Service, 18–19

ISBN 9781631439650
LCCN 2014959636

Printed in the United States of America
Mankato, MN
July, 2015
PA02264

ABOUT THE AUTHOR

Jody Jensen Shaffer is the author of 20 books of fiction and nonfiction for children. She also publishes poetry, stories, and articles in children's magazines. When not writing, Shaffer copyedits for children's publishers. She works from her home in Missouri, just east of the Great Plains.

TABLE OF CONTENTS

CHAPTER ONE

FRISKY FERRETS

Curious black-footed ferrets hunt on the prairie.

Up from a **prairie** den pops a little face with a black mask.
It is the face of a black-footed ferret. Its long, sleek body runs
through the grass. The ferret is hunting for its next meal.

The black-footed ferret is part of the weasel family.
Weasels are **mammals**. Otters, badgers, and wolverines

are also in the weasel family. The black-footed ferret is the only ferret native to North America. It is different from pet ferrets. Those come from a European type of weasel.

The ferret's long, thin body has short legs and strong claws. Much of its fur is tan. It has black fur on its legs, tail, and feet. Black also forms a mask shape on its face.

Black-footed ferrets live on the prairies of South Dakota.

Black-footed ferrets are close to 6 inches (15 cm) tall. They are 18 to 24 inches (46 to 61 cm) from head to tail. The ferrets weigh between 1.5 and 2.5 pounds (.7 and 1.1 kg). Males are bigger than females.

Black-footed ferrets live on the prairie. They once lived in areas from southern Canada to northern Mexico. Today black-footed ferrets live in just 21 places in the United States. These are areas where scientists have returned ferrets to the wild.

This black-footed ferret's sharp eyes look out from its black mask.

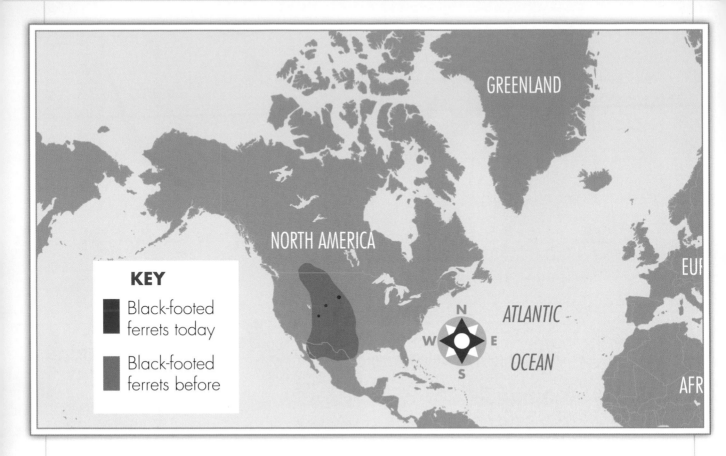

KEY

Black-footed ferrets today

Black-footed ferrets before

GREENLAND

NORTH AMERICA

ATLANTIC

OCEAN

EUF

AFR

Range of the black-footed ferret in the wild

The ferrets spend most of their time below ground. They eat, sleep, and raise their young in dens. The dens are called burrows. The ferrets leave their burrows at night to hunt.

Black-footed ferrets are carnivores. Prairie dogs are their main food. The ferrets also eat ground squirrels, rabbits, and birds. Ferrets store and eat their food underground. They steal underground burrows from prairie dogs. This protects them from **predators** as they eat. Foxes, coyotes, owls, and golden eagles all hunt black-footed ferrets.

Living underground also protects black-footed ferret babies. Baby ferrets are called kits. Black-footed ferrets mate in the spring. In May or June, three or four kits are born.

DO THE FERRET!

Black-footed ferrets are very playful and curious. Sometimes young ferrets do a special dance. With mouths wide open, they hop, leap, and kick their back legs. They leap out of their burrows and dive back into them again. They arch their backs like a scared cat. They hop so all four feet are off the ground at the same time.

They are blind and helpless. Kits stay underground until they are two months old. Then their mother takes them on hunting trips. At six months old, the kits move out. They find a new home. They hunt in a different part of the prairie. At a year old, females can have kits of their own.

Black-footed ferrets are very rare animals. Some scientists consider them the rarest animal in North America. They were once almost **extinct**. But now their numbers are coming back. There is hope for this animal's future.

**Ferret kits grow quickly and live on their own
by the time they are six months old.**

CHAPTER TWO

ALMOST EXTINCT

Settlers changed the look of the prairie and destroyed prairie dog habitat.

The black-footed ferret is an **endangered** animal. As the prairie dog's **habitat** has been taken away, ferrets have had a lot less food to eat.

Many years ago, prairie dogs were very common. Hundreds of millions lived across the North American prairie. Tens of thousands of black-footed ferrets lived there, too.

Around 1900, **pioneers** moved to the prairie. They wanted to grow crops. They hoped to raise cattle and other livestock, too. Farmers and ranchers thought prairie dogs were pests. Farmers plowed up their burrows. Ranchers fenced off land. People shot and poisoned the prairie dogs.

Many prairie dogs died off. Black-footed ferrets lost their food supply. They lost their burrows, too. The ferrets died in large numbers. By the late 1950s, people thought black-footed ferrets were extinct.

Prairie dogs provide food and homes for black-footed ferrets.

Black-footed ferrets also died for other reasons. Many suffered from disease. Flies spread a **plague**. The plague killed most of the ferrets that got it. It killed many prairie dogs, too. Another virus that causes fever and other serious health problems killed thousands of ferrets. Ferrets also died from **parasites**.

In 1964, an exciting thing happened. Scientists found a small group of black-footed ferrets in South Dakota. Three years later, they listed the species as endangered. They hoped to find more black-footed ferrets. But the South Dakota ferrets began to die. Scientists captured nine of them. They hoped to **breed** more in labs. But by 1979, all these ferrets had died, too. Scientists feared the ferrets were extinct. A few years later, a Wyoming ranch dog changed everything. In 1981

SPOTLIGHTING

Scientists use a method to count black-footed ferrets. It is called spotlighting. The searches take place at night. That is when the ferrets are most active. Searchers use large spotlights so they can see the ferrets. They shine their lights on burrow holes. When ferrets pop out, the light reflects in the ferrets' eyes. Searchers can count them.

Scientists use spotlights to see ferrets pop out of their burrows at night.

he brought home a dead black-footed ferret. Scientists knew finding a dead ferret meant there were probably live ones nearby, too. Five years later, scientists captured the wild ferrets to breed them in labs. By 1987 there were only 18 black-footed ferrets left in the world.

CHAPTER THREE

BACK ON THE PRAIRIE

Black-footed ferrets are getting help from scientists.

Scientists have done a lot to help black-footed ferrets. They did not know much about the ferrets when they captured them in 1987. They studied the animals to learn how they lived.

Environmental groups are saving black-footed ferret habitat.

The scientists learned how ferrets raised families. They started to breed ferrets in labs across the United States.

More than 8,000 black-footed ferrets have been born in labs. Scientists have released 3,500 into the wild. Some of those ferrets died. In 2013, between 500 and 1,000 ferrets still lived in the wild. Three hundred more were in labs. They were getting ready to be released.

Breeding ferrets in labs was a success. But scientists still had a problem. There were not enough wild prairie dogs to feed the ferrets. Many prairie dog homes had been destroyed. To help the ferrets, scientists had to help prairie dogs, too.

People are doing many things to save prairie dogs. Prairie dogs have been moved to new areas where their habitats are safe. They have started new burrows. Those burrows are alive with activity.

Scientists make sure ferrets are healthy and protected from disease before releasing them into the wild.

People also went to court to save prairie dogs. They helped get rid of an old Kansas law. It said ranchers had to kill prairie dogs. Also, an environmental group purchased land in South Dakota where prairie dogs live. The group hopes protecting the land will increase the number of prairie dogs. Increasing their numbers should increase the number of black-footed ferrets, too.

Scientists also want to help keep black-footed ferrets healthy. They have created **vaccines**. One helps fight plague. It is given to ferrets as a shot. Scientists give the vaccine to all

LEARNING TO HUNT

The first black-footed ferrets bred in labs died when they were released into the wild. They did not know how to hunt prairie dogs. They did not know how to survive on their own. Now, before being released, black-footed ferrets are put in outdoor pens where prairie dogs live. Here ferrets have a safe place to learn to hunt. Then they are released into the wild.

ferrets born in labs. Burrows are also dusted with chemicals. They kill the fleas that spread plague.

The number of wild black-footed ferrets is rising. These animals are once again dancing on the prairie.

The number of ferrets bred in labs has grown since 1989.

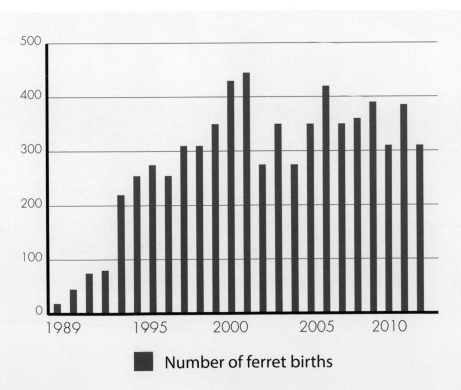

Number of ferret births

WHAT YOU CAN DO

- Find a zoo that has a black-footed ferret or prairie dog exhibit. Learn all you can.

- Tell your classmates and friends about the endangered black-footed ferret.

- Write a letter to your senators or representatives. Tell them about black-footed ferrets. Encourage them to save prairie dog habitats in your state.

GLOSSARY

breed (BREED) To breed is to keep animals so that you can produce more of them. Scientists breed black-footed ferrets in labs.

endangered (en-DANE-jerd) An endangered animal is in danger of becoming extinct. Black-footed ferrets are endangered.

extinct (ek-STINKT) If a type of animal is extinct, all the animals have died out. Many people believed the black-footed ferret had become extinct.

habitat (HAB-i-tat) A habitat is a place where an animal lives. Prairie dogs and black-footed ferrets share a habitat.

mammals (MAM-alz) Mammals are animals that are warm-blooded, give birth to live young, and are usually covered with hair. Black-footed ferrets are mammals.

parasites (PAR-a-sites) Parasites are living things that feed on other living things. Black-footed ferrets can get sick if they have parasites.

pioneers (pye-uh-NEERZ) Pioneers are people who go somewhere first, opening that place up for others. Pioneers moved to the Great Plains to farm and raise cattle and other livestock.

plague (PLAYG) A plague is a disease that causes a high rate of death. Plague kills many black-footed ferrets.

prairie (PRAYR-ee) A prairie is a large area of mostly grassland. The Great Plains is a prairie.

predators (PRED-a-terz) Predators hunt, kill, and eat other animals. Black-footed ferrets have several predators in the wild.

vaccines (vak-SEENZ) Vaccines help animals fight diseases. Vaccines for plague and other diseases help keep black-footed ferrets healthy.

TO LEARN MORE

BOOKS

Animals Alive. New York: DK Publishing, 2011.

Aronin, Miriam. *Black-Footed Ferrets: Back from the Brink.* New York: Bearport, 2008.

Hoare, Ben, and Tom Jackson. *Endangered Animals.* New York: DK Publishing, 2010.

Patkau, Karen. *Who Needs a Prairie? A Grassland Ecosystem.* Plattsburgh, NY: Tundra Books of Northern New York, 2014.

WEB SITES

Visit our Web site for links about black-footed ferrets:
childsworld.com/links

Note to Parents, Teachers, and Librarians: We routinely verify our Web links to make sure they are safe and active sites. So encourage your readers to check them out!

INDEX